After Iris,
and Other Poems

by

Jay Appleton

Wildhern Press 2011

Published by
Wildhern Press

Echo Library
Unit 22
Horcott Industrial Estate
Horcott Road
Fairford
Glos. GL7 4BX

www.echo-library.com

Please report serious faults in the text to
complaints@echo-library.com

ISBN 978-1-84830-336-2

AFTER IRIS, AND OTHER POEMS

By

JAY APPLETON

CONTENTS

£6

AFTER IRIS

It's Hallowe'en.
What does that really mean?
Each year we tolerate the same old scene:
All down the street
Nothing but 'trick or treat',
Pumpkins aflame; ghosts in a flapping sheet!

It's such a bore;
I've seen it all before.
I don't think I can take it any more!
It's not for me,
This flippant levity.
I'm wrestling with a different memory.

Four years today
Since Iris passed away!
Re-visiting that inauspicious day
Opens a train
Of memories again,
A search for sunshine following the rain.

When marriage ends
It's then one turns to friends,
And only then one really comprehends
The debt one owes
To all the folk one knows
And, if one's lucky, that's the way it goes!

Four years ago
I didn't really know
How to recover from that bitter blow,
But soon I found
My friends had rallied round
And once again life's pleasures now abound.

Mercifully
I have a family
Deeply committed to look after me.
They don't live near,
Yet they are often here,
Some even from the Southern Hemisphere!

Lucky am I!
I often wonder why
After bereavement some don't even try
To face the strife,
With no supporting wife,
Of taking steps to get another life.

Of course we miss
That fond connubial kiss
Which through the years has symbolized
     our bliss,
But once we know
Those days have had to go,
It's useless to pretend it isn't so.

So while I may
Still dream of yesterday,
Plans for tomorrow still come into play.
And now, for me,
My creativity
Is satisfied in writing poetry.

That wasn't what

Was ever in the plot,

But now I'm spending time on it a lot,

So this is me

Using my poetry

To urge a positive philosophy.

BEWILDERING BIBLICAL BRIEFINGS

It doesn't do for us to imitate
All of the precedents the Scriptures state.
Some stories in the Bible seem to be
In flagrant conflict with morality.
The sort of God who ordered Abraham
To offer up a sacrificial lamb,
But only when the process had begun
Of coldly butchering his helpless son,
Is not the sort of caring deity
Likely to kindle much respect in me.
A civilised society today
Would tell the story in a different way.
Isaac would obviously then and there
Be summarily taken into care,
Being a child at risk of an attack
By an extreme religious maniac.
God's chief pre-occupation was to know
How far the father was prepared to go
In mindlessly consenting to destroy
The life of a confused, bewildered boy.

This God, it seemed, was more content to be
Assured of his lieutenant's loyalty
Than mercifully thinking of the lad
Who obviously had done nothing bad.
Abraham, one would think, could hardly fail
To earn himself a tidy stretch in gaol.
What sort of message does this story tell?
It's less to do with Heaven than with Hell.
The Holy Scriptures must be subject to
The cleansing wind of critical review.
Stories which edify we should contrive
By all within our power to keep alive,
But where their moral meaning is in doubt
We shouldn't hesitate to sling 'em out!

BLAKEMERE

Two processes, the one immensely slow,
The other over in an hour or so!

Picture this place ten thousand years ago,
Treeless and bleak and carpeted with snow,
Whose cumulative pressure will suffice
To turn its lower layers into ice.
It leaves behind it, as it melts away,
Patches of gravel, sand and boulder-clay.
Among this glacial residue you'll find
Clusters of small depressions left behind,
Which fill with water, and around the edge
Acquire a fringe of rushes, sand and sedge.
In some of these the process is complete.
What once were lakelets now are swathes
    of peat,
Surfaces firm enough to walk across
On Bettisfield and Fenn's and Whixall Moss.
In others, though, up to the present day,
Post-glacial water-bodies hold at bay

This colonising vegetation, and
Slow down the change from water into land.
Near Ellesmere now such lakelets form a chain
Of glistening jewels in the Shropshire Plain,
Catching the eye especially where these
Enjoy protection from encircling trees.
The image of that former frozen waste
Has now been almost totally effaced,
And friendly water-surfaces appear
Backed by a blend of oak and conifer.
How fitting that one magic little lake
Should bear the honourable name of Blake,
Who, in his pictures and his poetry,
Focussed attention on to 'mystery'!
For as we sit in readiness to pay
Romantic homage to the dying day,
The power of 'feeling' now takes precedence
Over that rational intelligence
Which through the day has guided us afloat
Safe in the confines of our narrowboat,
Now moored securely and in easy reach
Of where we're gathered on this sheltered beach
To watch the fading panorama and
Delight in things we may not understand.

The calm reflective water by-and-by
Picks out the pastel colours of the sky
Where thin translucent clouds of palest pink
Watch the descending Sun-god slowly sink
Behind that leafy, dense arboreal screen
Of life-creating chlorophyllic green.
This demonstration we have just been through,
Within the compass of an hour or two,
Which takes the rainbow colours of the day
And slowly strips their brilliance away,
Is not unlike a sort of parody
Of what transpired in the Quaternary.
What happened in the twinkling of an eye,
Briefly enacted in the Shropshire sky,
Mimics that saga of ten thousand years
In which a glacial landscape disappears,
Except that, while our evening picture-show
Told how the friendly scene was doomed to go,
The ice-sheet of our ancient heritage
Has been re-clothed in friendlier foliage;
The daytime chorus of the waterfowl
Is heard no more, and as the tawny owl
Flutes its farewell to the fast-fading light,
We'll to the cosy longboat for the night!

THE BLUE MOUNTAINS

Hawkesbury Sandstone was the famous name
Chosen by English Colonists who came
To occupy those new-discovered lands
On which the Sydney conurbation stands.
The finest anchorage in New South Wales
Was flanked by local spreads of fertile shales
Which gave the settlers opportunities
To grow their day-to-day necessities.
But, as the early population grew,
They felt the need to search for pastures new.
A massive sheet of arenaceous rock
Beyond the settled land sufficed to block
The path of any grazier who tried
To find fresh grasslands on the other side.
Every adventurer was at a loss
To find a practicable way across
Those vertical, impenetrable walls
Of precipices, cliffs and waterfalls.
Every attempt to cross them was in vain;
Hawkesbury Sandstone drove them back again.

To them it seemed a sort of prison wall
With no redeeming properties at all,
A place devoid of opportunity,
Steeped in an aura of hostility.

*   *   *

This image of an area accursed
Has now spectacularly been reversed
As Sydneysiders daily flock to see
The pageant of its stunning scenery,
Which steals the vibrant, penetrating light
To paint its face with mottled pink and white,
While managing to keep that hazy hue
Of all-pervading toponymic 'Blue'.
In recent years the botanists have found
New species in this forest-covered ground.
Masked in a cloak of chlorophyllic green
Which overlies the shaley Narrabeen,
Secreted imperceptibly away
Where nature still holds undisputed sway.

Those colonists, so painfully distressed
To find themselves excluded from the West,
Could not have known the rock that barred their
way
Would so delight their progeny today.

BUTTONOLOGY

The button was a primitive device
That solved a lady's problems in a trice.
It meant that she could fasten up her dress
In freedom from anxiety and stress.
But handling buttons, to a simple male,
Presents a challenge well beyond the pale.
'Buttonhole' is a word that doesn't fit.
It's not a hole at all; more like a slit.
While men in general are thought to be
Better at managing technology,
It ought to be a pretty simple goal
To push a button through a buttonhole.
Yet I can spend forever getting cross
Trying to show the button who's the boss.
A rumour circulating through the land
Promised that help would shortly be at hand.
For men this was a long-awaited prize:
No more embarrassment about our flies!
What superseded this sartorial curse
Was soon to prove incomparably worse!

This brainchild of some brain-deficient berk
For me invariably fails to work.
It's always *I* who seem to have the luck
Somehow to get the damned contraption stuck.
It won't pull up and yet it won't pull down.
So if you see me walking round the town
All unabashed and with my flies undone,
You'll know I've given up.   The zip has won!

CARRY ON WALKING

To Julia Bradbury, President of *The Ramblers*

The knowledge that a couplet which I wrote
Seems to have struck a sympathetic note
Emboldens me to say in poetry
Thanks for the pleasure you have given me,
Walking with Alfred Wainwright, mile by mile,
And now on the updated *Countryfile*,
With many a lively programme in between
Enlivening my television screen.
I've followed you by railways and canals,
By lakes and mountain peaks and waterfalls,
And as you roam the country, everywhere
You make me feel that I am really there.
My walking boots were getting old and worn
On railway tracks when you were still unborn.
It was indulging in this favourite sport
Led me to write the Appleton Report
Which curbed the sale of railway property
And saved the trackbed for posterity.

Old men with the presumption to engage
With ladies clearly less than half their age
Should be regarded most suspiciously;
They are the stock-in-trade of comedy.
Figures like Don Pasquale ought to know
Far better; so should Doctor Bartolo,
And, never mind the mischief they intend,
They all get their come-uppance in the end!
But I assure you I am far enough
From all that comic-operatic stuff,
Then there's the safety net to intervene -
I mean, of course, the television screen,
Offering you a cast-iron guarantee
Against uncalled-for impropriety!
Yours are the feet to guide me far and wide
Across the charismatic countryside;
Yours are the eyes through which I still can see
The beauties of its stunning scenery.
Carry on walking over hill and vale;
You stride ahead and I'll bring up the tail.
Together we will sniff the morning air.
You'll never notice me, but I'll be there!

CARTESIAN CONUNDRUM

The bodies that we occupy,
    Our shells of flesh and bone,
We think of as our property,
    As ours and ours alone;
    Yet they are not our own!

The atoms and the molecules
    Which I regard as 'me',
Will in the crematorium
    Achieve their liberty.
    The fire will set them free.

Descartes was right when he declared
    'Cogito ergo sum',
But when the Terminator comes
    And strikes me deaf and dumb
    What will I then become?

Cartesian philosophy
  No longer will apply,
For I will cease to cogitate
    The moment that I die
    However hard I try.

The usage of the present tense
    Implies I still exist,
Yet if you tried to find me on
    The 'living persons' list,
    You'd find my name was missed.

So in that Latin *dictum* which
    Established that 'I am'
We must delete that '*ergo sum*'
    Out of the epigram
    And substitute '*eram*'!

CAT-A-WALLING

Beside my garden there's a little wall,
I guess approximately six feet tall,
And on the top a pair of cats parade;
One's black and white, the other's marmalade.
They're very well-behaved; they never fight.
They seem to share the territorial right
To pace the garden wall from end to end
Like sentries under orders to defend
The borders of my humble property.
But what, I'm bound to say, amazes me,
Is how they keep their distance when they're
    there;
They're never seen together as a pair.
It's quite uncanny how they seem to learn
To organise their duties turn-by-turn.
Is it instinctive that they seem to know
When it's the time for them to have a go?
Do they 'relieve' each other, so to speak,
And if, in doing so, is this unique?

It isn't rocket science for a man
To set in hand a proper rota-plan,
But can a cat aspire to know the way
To organise a rota day by day?
So does this mean we haven't had the sense
To recognise feline intelligence,
And is our human right to dominate
The feline world, which we've assumed to date,
Illusory?   Are we in jeopardy
Of feline-dominant *cat*astrophe?

CHAUVINISTIC TRAINS

Tank Engine Thomas has to share the blame
For giving man a chauvinistic name.
Dragging his train of wretched concubines
Hither and thither down the railway lines,
Repeatedly, as Mr Awdry showed,
The engine ruled his meek, subservient load
Of ill-contented carriages, required
To follow him wherever he desired.
Annie and Clarabel, his harassed wives,
Suffered the most uncomfortable lives
As servile and submissive rolling-stock
Complying with his orders round the clock.
Edward and Gordon?   They were just as bad,
Ill-treating all the carriages they had,
Bumping them roughly till their bumpers hurt,
Treating their wagons like a load of dirt.
This ruthless domination by the male
Suggests out-dated values still prevail.

It is an image that we must reject,

Politically *very* incorrect,

A despicably ill-considered plan

To justify the primacy of man.

But Mr Awdry, when he came along,

Very embarrassingly got it wrong!

Don't buy this plug for masculinity.

A locomotive's *always* known as SHE!

CON

In Memoriam, M. R. G. Conzen.

We walked the hills of Shropshire
    With Conzen at our side,
Our charismatic teacher,
        Our mentor and our guide,
        Our questions satisfied.

We sauntered down the Onny
    To where it joins the Teme,
We watched its waters winding
        Towards its distant dream
        Of reaching Severn's stream.

In the quaint streets of Ludlow
    He'd take the map apart,
Explaining every detail,
        The master of his art,
        And won this student's heart.

Beginning with the *Landschaft*
    He taught us how to see.
This was my introduction
    To true geography,
    The gift he gave to me.

Each time I take the railway
    From Hereford to Crewe
I re-explore that landscape
    As I am passing through,
    Re-living it anew.

His seminars are over,
    His teaching days are done,
But still in us, his pupils,
    His thinking carries on.
    We'll not forget you, Con!

THE DAME GAME

Heroes like Newton, Churchill, Galahad,
Who added titles to the names they had,
Be they eccentric, drunk or even mad,
Cannot, we think, be altogether bad.

For anyone, I guess, the prefix 'Sir'
Is pretty well assured to cause a stir,
But, should he change his gender, as it were,
What could the Heralds' College do for *her*?

Suppose we wish to treat a girl the same
By grafting on a handle to her name,
It seems to me a lamentable shame
Our only option is to call her 'Dame'.

While 'Sir' recalls the days when knights
       were bold,
A dame's a sheep from quite another fold.
She's pantomimic, ugly, fat and old,
Cast in a vulgar 'Widow Twanky' mould.

It surely is a veritable crime
To honour heroines from time to time
By using words which ought to be sublime
Straight from the language of the pantomime.

The heroines we choose to emulate
Must be deserving of a better fate.
We need a title more appropriate
For women whom we wish to venerate.

All sorts of neutral titles come to mind
Which are conveniently gender-blind.
It surely should be possible to find
Something more flattering to womankind!

Doctors, professors, judges and the rest
Are used to being sexlessly addressed
By forms of style and title which suggest
The various professions they've professed.

Simply to add the common suffix, '-ess',
Will rarely prove the way to solve the mess.
Though 'mister' may convert to 'misteress',
It still occasions some uneasiness!

So in the future when it's time for us
To praise the feminine illustrious,
Let some bright spark, young and ingenious,
Come up with something more mellifluous!

EAST AND WEST

Oh, East is East, and West is West,
And never the twain shall meet.

Rudyard Kipling

Our eastern and our western coastlines are
In their geology dissimilar,
So, too, the music I associate
With each of them is often disparate.
The differences in their scenery
Call for a different musicality.
The Mesozoic and Quaternary
Confront the challenge of the eastern sea,
Where only intermittent cliffs display
Relief from sandy dunes or boulder-clay,
Which seem to find their true expression in
The gentle music of the violin.
The western fringes of the continent
Call for a wider choice of instrument.
It's true that, when the savage tempest roars
And with malicious might assaults our shores,

Brass and percussion come into their own;
Eastern and western shores behave as one.
But when the wild tempestuous weather clears
Then the distinction quickly re-appears.
The lonely harpist on the mountain slope,
Mixing her recipe of tears and hope,
A soulful, melancholy melody
In the inevitable minor key,
Would be incongruously out of place
On the smooth sweep of England's eastern face.
Transplanted from her native Celtic land,
She'd never thrive on miles of golden sand.
To feed her brand of musical romance
She needs a Palaeozoic provenance,
Some rough and rugged rock on which to sit
And coax sublime *arpeggios* out of it.
So each of us, as we experience
Manifestations of this difference,
Will personally forge a link which binds
Music to favourite places in our minds.
Such links, which others may find hard to see,
Become for each of us reality.

Music, downloaded on our mental screen,

Recalling visions of some coastal scene,

Will, in the context of geography,

Thus vindicate Kipling's duality.

ELEGIAC EXPERIMENT

(A testpiece to see whether the metre of Latin elegiac couplets is incompatible with the rhythms of the English language, as is often suggested. Rhyme, of course, is not used in the Latin, but is obviously required here.)

This was the lonely place where the night and
        the morning were meeting.
   Down went the moon in the west,
   Slowly retiring to rest.
Acres of open space, as the worn-out night was
        retreating
   Welcomed the newborn day,
   Brushing the darkness away.

Plenty to challenge the eye as the sun came up
        with the morning;
   Loneliness far and wide
   Stretching on every side.

Lurid streaks in the sky, the shepherd's
proverbial warning,
Flashing a signal of red,
Told of disturbance ahead.

Over the moors he went while avidly keeping
his eyes on
That riveting ribbon of road
Down which he purposely strode.
On with redoubled intent he made for the
distant horizon
Summoning him away
Into the brightening day.

Nothing there was to engender concern or
suppressed agitation,
Only the freedom to roam,
Cheerfully sauntering home.
All that it took to espouse a sense of
expectant elation,
Linked to the beat of a song,
Stubbornly drove him along.

Then at the brow of a hill the prospect that
opened before him
Signalled the message that here
Comfort and welcome were near.
So with an effort of will and the promise of
home to restore him
Now was the time to descend
Where his adventure would end.

Entering into the street, and aware of the
houses enclosing,
Soon he was pondering on
Where all the distance had gone.
Homecoming now was a treat and he relished
the thought of reposing.
Wiser, he now could see
Just what it means to be free!

ePENFRIENDS

I'm getting old.   The parts are wearing out.
I find it difficult to get about.
I must accept my geriatric state
Because I know I'm past my sell-by date.
But 'golden oldies' who are really smart
Now use the electronic counterpart
Of what we had for letter-writing when
We'd nothing better than the fountain-pen.
For us the email clearly is the way
To hold the march of decadence at bay.
It's the computer which enables me
To contact penfriends so successfully.
I know it's too ridiculous for words,
But yes, at ninety, I'm still pulling birds!

EVE

Evil is all the fault of womankind.
The Book of Genesis has told us so.
It was Eve's treachery which undermined
Adam's pathetic stance so long ago.
All sorts of consequences lay in store.
Serpents have paid the price by eating dust;
We men are doomed to toil for evermore.
Women, predictably, have lost our trust.
The monstrous regiment of women now
Disclaim responsibility for sin.
Eve, they insist, is not to blame, and how
Disastrous is the mess *that* leaves us in?
Their fury is a terrifying sight,
Not least because they're obviously right!

FRITZ

The rain was falling from a leaden sky,
And in the Nissen hut were Fritz and I.
Fritz was today abnormally subdued,
In a dejected, melancholy mood.
Now that the active fighting was complete,
Before we could return to Civvy Street,
Some added personnel were needed for
Running the camps for prisoners of war
Who, being still regarded as the foe,
Were held here for another year or so.
Though still supposed to be my enemy,
Fritz never showed me animosity.
The Army Regulations made it clear
There was to be no 'fraternising' here.
We never must forget the fact that he
Was all the time subordinate to me.
Subject to that we had to find a way
To rub along together day by day,
And in a mood of mutual tolerance
He always showed a cheerful countenance.

Today, however, this was not the case.
I instantly detected in his face
The signs of some severe anxiety
Which he was hesitant to share with me.
Such was the measure of his private grief
He sat there sobbing in a handkerchief.
On this grim winter morning there we sat,
But what, I wondered, was he sobbing at?
I'd never seen a German soldier cry,
So rather sheepishly I caught his eye.
He never spoke a word, but presently
He pushed an 'aerogram' across to me,
In which a rough, untidy German hand
Told me enough for me to understand.
Each morning he'd re-organise anew
Things he required for what he had to do.
Characteristic German thoroughness
Ensured his desk was never in a mess,
And every day he'd find a special place
To stand a photo of his daughter's face.
She was the apple of her father's eye,
The homing beacon he was guided by.
She'd passed her seventh birthday in the spring
And was indeed a pretty little thing.

Last week, emerging from the factory gate
A lorry driver noticed her too late,
And in this crumpled aerogram I read
Little Brigitte Mittelbach was dead.
Can you conceive, supposing it were you,
What Fritz, her father, would be going through?
In this, the saddest moment of his life,
God knows what it was doing to his wife!
Work was unthinkable; he tried instead
To reconstruct a picture in his head.
He saw her there, determined to be brave,
Standing beside a gaping, empty grave.
She'd watched Brigitte lowered in the ground,
But why was Fritz, her father, not around?
To satisfy Fate's most vindictive whim,
He wasn't there when she most needed him.
I represented the authority
That held him back from where he ought to be.
This horror story left me unprepared.
I felt a sort of guilt that I'd been spared
The tribulation he had suffered here,
Unreachable by those who held him dear.
For me this was an ordinary day,
Just working out the prisoners' 'token pay'.

I stood and watched my prisoner where he sat,
Mocked by the figures he was staring at.
The columns that he should be adding up
Had, by the poison in his bitter cup,
Become transmuted into coils of rope
To strangle instantly that gleam of hope
That, when he surfaced from this vale of pain,
He'd hold Brigitte in his arms again.
Though obviously I could not be blamed,
Yet, notwithstanding that, I felt ashamed!
Over the months Fritz had become my friend
And here was I, unable to extend
The sort of help he needed.   It was I
Who symbolised for him the reason why
He wasn't with her when Brigitte died.
It was no wonder that he sat and cried.
Because I'd failed my friend, a sense of shame
Coursed through my body like a cleansing flame,
And life for me would never be the same.

GUANTANAMO BAY

Millions of decent people never saw
How disingenuous it was to foil
The tiresome strictures of the U. S. law
By moving everything to Cuban soil.
Rendition, waterboarding and the rest,
Infringing human rights in various ways,
Were meant to find acceptance when expressed
In neutral, less disturbing turns of phrase.
But in a so-called democratic state
It surely should have been *our* job to know,
And passionately seek to remonstrate
At what was brewing in Guantanamo.
Who were these ostriches who wouldn't see?
Well, one of them, I have to say, was me!

GRADUATION DAY

A thought occurred to me the other day,
Namely, that university degrees
Are like a garden path that leads the way
Through flowers, bushes, shrubberies and trees.
It's not the path itself we come to see,
It's paving stones, its gravel or its grass,
Nor, when evaluating a Degree,
Should we be looking only at its Class.
The garden path provides us with a kind
Of viewpoint for what lies on either side.
It's in its flanking margins that we find
Aesthetic aspirations satisfied.
The crude assessments which exams provide
Focus attention on the paths we took;
The haunts we visited on either side,
Those are the places where we ought to look.
What we should prize on Graduation Day,
What should be most important, is the view
Of *all* that we've encountered on the way,
Not just the steps themselves which brought us
    through.

THE HIGHWAYMAN

No weapon was he brandishing,
    No pistol in his hand.
That didn't stop him uttering
    His sinister command.

The travellers, predictably,
    Were frankly terrified.
The man reacted angrily,
    The lady simply cried.

'Don't worry!' said the highwayman,
    'I am not even armed.
'I'm just a country gentleman,
    'You'll go away unharmed.

'I stopped the coach to ask the way
    'To Market Lavington.
'Your coachman knows it, I dare say,
    'I'll ask him and be gone.

'I have a speech impediment
   'Which causes me distress,
'But I am the embodiment
   'Of gentle friendliness.

'So do not be alarmed, because
   'I'd never take your life.
'I just asked who the lady was,
   'Your mummy or your wife?'

IF ONLY

If Guido Fawkes had played his cards aright
We never would have had our Bonfire Night.
If Henry Tudor kept his cool instead
Of chopping off his royal spouse's head,
If Charlie Stuart, having spent the night
Encamped at Derby, hadn't taken fright
And hurried north with ignominious speed
To safer haunts beyond the River Tweed,
What might have happened to the Monarchy
Without a Hanoverian Dynasty?
If Wolf and Schubert were not so remiss
As to contract a dose of syphilis,
Just think of all the *lieder* there might be
Now bringing joy to their posterity,
And what a difference it might have made
If Beethoven had had a hearing-aid!
Had Christopher Columbus pressed his claim
To give America its rightful name,
If Adolf Hitler had been born a Jew,
Or Stalin died of cholera at two,

The world would be a different place today;
We'd have to throw the history books away.
If only, back in eighteen-twenty-three,
Webb-Ellis hadn't fouled disgracefully,
We never would have had the rugby game
And Welsh religion wouldn't be the same.
If only you had realised this rhyme
Would prove to be a useless waste of time

    . . . . . !

K.364

Beside the dying fire, and all alone,
I watched her peeping round the opening door,
And in the evening light the gramophone
Was playing Mozart's Koechel Three Six Four.

'What is the music, then?' she shyly said.
'Sinfonia Concertante' I replied.
We played it through before we went to bed,
Watching the flickering firelight, side by side.

We both were haunted by that melody,
Bewitched by Mozart's sorcery, and soon
This favourite from the eighteenth century
We had adopted as our 'Special Tune'.

It's strange what fantasies the brain invents
When sentiments of youthful love begin.
We soon *became* those solo instruments,
I the viola, she the violin.

One of the soloists would take the lead
Then hand it over to the other one.
That's how a pair of lovers *should* proceed,
Sharing the load until the task is done.

What does the Second Movement seem to say?
Starting and ending in a minor key,
Yet flirting with the major on the way?
'Unity forged out of diversity?'

So, in this matrimonial parody
We found a play reflecting married life,
And there, in counterpoint and harmony,
We heard the story of a man and wife.

Today, alas, my violin has gone
After a partnership of sixty years,
I, the viola, have to struggle on
Scorning the solace of consoling tears.

This afternoon that old familiar strain
Revived those feelings of togetherness.
I seemed to see us dancing once again,
Concelebrating lifelong happiness.

Was this the message Mozart had in mind,
Blending the voices of each instrument,
In a romantic partnership combined,
So much alike and yet so different?

THE LAST CLIMB

High up the mountain path I tread,
　　And for a yard or two
The rising ground which lies ahead
　　Still terminates the view.

Behind my back the countryside,
　　Nature's great work of art,
Stretches my vision far and wide.
　　And captivates my heart.

There lie the moors, the hills, the trees,
　　The sights I have adored,
The archive where my memories
　　Are permanently stored.

I turn to cast a rueful eye
　　On where I once had been,
For soon it's time to say goodbye
　　To that nostalgic scene.

In front of me the skyline lies;
    I've nearly reached the top.
The path on which I'd set my eyes
    Seems suddenly to stop.

Although I can no longer see
    The path which lies ahead,
Imagination still is free
    To do the job instead.

Our lives are like that Lakeland climb
    Which scales that Lakeland fell,
As we approach our destined time
    To bid our last farewell.

The landscape we must leave behind
    Has been a lifelong friend.
Are there new landscapes still to find
    Beyond our journey's end?

LEICESTER LIMERICK

There was a young lady of Leicester
Who went on a visit to Cheicester.
    She arrived in the town
    With her pants hanging down
And a constable had to arreicester!

LITTLE GIRL[1]

I'm looking at her photo in a frame.
She wears an air of wistful innocence.
She has no notion yet of wealth or fame
Or what she may expect from Providence.
We, who will know her in her future years,
Already may with hindsight think we see
Signs of her hopes, her happiness, her fears,
In her emerging personality.
What does her coming childhood hold in store?
We cannot share those years which lie ahead.
Only through tales of what she'd done before
Can we recover what she did and said.
Here, on the very threshold of her life,
How could she know she was to be my wife?

---

[1] See Front Cover, Iris (née Hearn) at 6.

LOCKSLEY HALL

After parting from his soldier friends to lay his
    feelings bare,
Resurrecting bitter memories of anger and
    despair,

It was while he was reflecting on the passions of
    his youth
That he casually stumbled on this universal
    truth:

When reviewing the successes we've
    accomplished day by day,
We must not resent the failures we've
    encountered on the way,

For when anger is unbridled and when jealousy
    is rife
Then the poison of resentment can destroy a
    person's life.

It is prudent to be mindful, when we find
    ourselves distressed,
That what looked like a disaster may be really
    for the best.

We must somehow learn to handle
    disappointments, great or small,
For we each, if we are honest, have our secret
    Locksley Hall.

It's the place in which experience of love and
    ecstasy
Was replaced by the frustrations of a sad reality.

In the spring a young man's fancy lightly stole
    his heart away;
In the end the soldier's daydream led him back
    to yesterday.

If the many disappointments which in youth we
    have to face
Are allowed to keep in retrospect their
    unforgiving place,

If an unfulfilled ambition, left to fester in the
    mind
Can defy obliteration and be always left behind,

The ambitions that we cherished in our
    optimistic years
Will instead become the agents of our
    pessimistic fears.

In the cruel light of reason what eventually told
Was a father's disapproval and a rival's pot of
    gold,

So a premature elation now had ended in
    distress
As a passion for his cousin had dissolved in
    bitterness.

A cantankerous relationship had suddenly begun
Like an unpredicted thunderstorm extinguishing
    the sun.

He would lose no opportunity to vilify her name
And his attitude to Locksley Hall would never be
the same.

In the visionary picture of the future that he
dreamt
He presented his usurper as an object of
contempt

Who would bring his cousin misery and soon
begin to tire
Of that first imagined ecstasy that set her heart
on fire,

While the thought of Amy's motherhood now
chilled him to the bone,
As she lavished her affection on an infant not his
own!

Should he leave behind the prospect of an
orderly career?
Should he spoil the polished surface of its
cultural veneer?

Should he stoop to take a mistress from a
simple, savage race
If it ended in opprobrium, rejection and
disgrace?

But we need to persevere and read the story to
the end.
It is then we shall discover he is still prepared to
spend

Time to ponder implications of a new
philosophy
Based on visions of a better world of peace and
harmony.

There he looks with aspiration at a beatific scene
Where the squalid world is conquered by the
world that might have been.

Though his anger, unabated at the faithlessness
of love,
And the cynical betrayal he was still complaining
of,

Never wholly ceased to smoulder in his
    unforgiving heart,
It was now no more destroying him and tearing
    him apart.

We can deprecate the fury which his jealousy
    produced;
We can frown upon the way in which his lover
    was traduced,

But a more propitious vision was belatedly
    unfurled
In a panoramic picture of a more fraternal
    world,

Where the scandals of society were hopefully
    replaced
And the relics of injustice unreservedly effaced,

Where posterity should work towards a more
    propitious plan
That would place the scales of justice in a
    Parliament of Man.

So the soldier storyteller, now reviewing what
    had passed,
Tried to find a new perspective, more
    commendable, at last.

In the end it was the sounding of that martial
    bugle-call
That released him, disillusioned, from the spell
    of Locksley Hall.

McMENDELSSOHN

The Scottish Landscape haunted Mendelssohn
A hundred years before it haunted me,
Yet when I found those hills to walk upon
I'd never heard the Scottish Symphony.
That was a sound I later grafted on
With retrospective authenticity.

From Holyrood he ventured north to brave
The hazards of the Hebridean Sea.
Blasted by tempest, buffeted by wave,
Scorning its aura of hostility,
He stole the music out of Fingal's cave
And then encoded it for you and me.

Now, calling that romantic land to mind,
Something I regularly like to do,
No matter how I try, I always find
I cannot seem to separate the two.
Landscape and music are for me combined
To reconstruct a realistic view.

With Mendelssohn's originality
Now reinforcing childhood memories,
I bring to life the Scottish scenery
Between the Cheviots and the Hebrides.
In partnership they can enable me
To visit Scotland any time I please.

THE MIDDAY SCOT

Here am I, sitting on a valley side
Which overlooks the rural Upper Clyde
Whose serpentine meanders, glassy bright,
Reflect the penetrating autumn light.
Beside the margins of the lazy stream
The metals of the railway also gleam.
Along the U-shaped valley-floor it swerves,
But in much wider, more expansive curves.
Sweeping along the valley, side by side,
The railway and the adolescent Clyde
Act like a dancing partnership and please
The eye with matching sinuosities.
Passing through Elvanfoot and Abington,
They find an easy path to Lamington;
Thanks to a glacial legacy they squeeze
Through Ordovician Sedimentaries,
First gently deviating to the right,
Then bearing left and slinking out of sight.
It is as though the valley wide and deep,
Had settled down to take its midday sleep.

Now, far away, a plume of steam appears
As gentle whispers reach expectant ears.
A Lilliputian train is starting to
Make its appearance in the field of view.
Larger it grows, and I distinguish what
Can only be the southbound Midday Scot.
Stanier's skill and Crewe's technology
Combined in engineering artistry
To build this awesome elegant machine,
As fine an engine as I've ever seen.
A train of carriages in 'Midland Red'
With this Pacific steaming at its head,
Swings sharply up the valley to my right,
Catching the changing angle of the light.
The powerful, pounding punch of flashing steel
Connects the piston to the driving wheel
As Walschaerts crowns this festival of steam
By adding syncopation to the theme.
The heavy breathing of the steam released
Like the fierce snorting of a wounded beast,
The regular, repeating, rhythmic 'clack'
Of bogies passing over jointed track,

Together these ingredients contrive
To prove this apparition is alive.
And now, to energise this living beast,
Its boiler pressure has to be increased
To overcome that final hundred feet
And make the climb of Beattock Bank complete.
The silvered trailing tresses it displays
Turn into dark, intimidating greys,
Which tell us a replenishment of coal
Was needed to achieve that final goal.
The sharp *staccato* of exhausted steam
Lends substance to this animistic dream
And for a moment leaves me wondering
How can one doubt it is a living thing?
In recollection I can see it still
Now slowly disappearing round a hill,
As, with its smoke still hanging in the sky,
Its parting whistle bids a faint 'Goodbye!'

NIGHT AND DAY

It tells us in the Book of Holy Writ
That God divided up the day and night.
He made a pretty decent job of it
And as a child I thought He got it right.
The time available for me to play
Was just enough to let me have my head.
However, by the ending of the day
I knew that I was ready for my bed.
But now I'm in my second infancy
I tend to think perhaps He got it wrong,
And, looking at it quite impartially,
The day for me is quite a bit too long.
As for the remedy, the thing to do
Is take a nap and chop the day in two.

NURSES

It's part of every nurse's expertise
To cope with all eventualities.
The worst she has to tolerate is when
She has to deal with chauvinistic men
Who think it natural to rule the lives
Of meek submissive, uncomplaining wives
And reckon it undignified to be
Subject to feminine authority.
Nurses are there to pamper them, and all
Are permanently at their beck and call.
Doctors' instructions they regard as what
The patient's free to carry out - or not,
And they resent the domineering way
Nurses expect their patients to obey.
But we who tread with equanimity
The path that leads us back to infancy,
That state of impotent dependence where
We all submitted to a woman's care,
We relish once again the luxury
Of leaving things to femininity.

Released from all the chores of every day.

We shamelessly enjoy the lazy way.

So, nurses, we salute you, one and all,

The guardian angels of the hospital!

OH WHAT A LOVELY DAY!

It is such a lovely morning
    With a lovely distant view,
And the far-off hills are shining
    In their pastel shades of blue.
On the hill where I am standing
    There is magic in the air,
In my heart I have a feeling
    It is Heaven everywhere.
I have racked my brains enquiring
    What's the cause of all my bliss?
Is it *just* a lovely morning
    That has made me feel like this?
Can there be some gland secreting
    Something alien in the blood
Surreptitiously disturbing
    What I thought understood?
Was it what I ate this morning?
    What I dreamt about last night?
Should I really find alarming
    What's about to come to light?

Is it some initial warning

    That I'm slowly going mad?

Is it some genetic failing

    I've inherited from Dad?

But it's time to stop enquiring

    What's the cause of it, because

I've begun to think this morning

    Not as lovely as it was!

ON NOT HITTING KIDS

There's one thing I have never understood,
How hitting kids will somehow make them
    good!
This was brought home to me the other day,
When I was slowly plodding up the brae.
Hearing an agitated infant cry,
I went to ascertain the reason why.
I saw a woman, resolute and grim,
Presumably his mother, hitting him,
So, pausing as I passed the garden gate,
I took it on myself to remonstrate.
Said she, 'All right for you to talk like that!
'Nobody can control the little brat!
'He never can behave himself for long.
'Somebody's got to teach him right from wrong!'
After a brief reflection I replied,
'Perhaps you ought to hear the other side.
'How can we teach our children that we need
'To banish violence in word and deed
'If we insist that we retain its use
'To force compliance any time we choose?

'Bright children won't take very long to see
'Through such a gross illogicality.
'Why should they follow what we try to teach
'Unless they see we practise what we preach?'
Surely it must be we who are at fault,
Condoning licensed physical assault!

THE PALAEOZOIC SUCCESSION

That outpost of the Carboniferous
Which Housman calls 'the purple head of Clee'
Starts a stratigraphy continuous
Right to the margin of the Irish Sea.
The Old Red Sandstone brings a ruddy hue
Exemplified in Herefordshire's vales.
The countryside Kilvert and Housman knew
Is like a sort of anteroom to Wales.
The layered rocks of the Silurian,
Clays in each tough and limestones on each
    crest,
Mimic the older Ordovician
Which underlies them further to the west.
From Shropshire, where we met this sequence
    first,
Almost to Life's primordial ancient home,
We find the order suddenly reversed.
We've reached at last the Cambrian Harlech
    Dome.

PARALLEL ROADS

Most children are committed to a view
Indoctrinated by the age of two,
And, not yet skilled in independent thought,
They have to swallow everything they're taught
About obedience to the discipline
Of the society they're living in.
It's not surprising, in those early years,
Before the power of reasoning appears,
That their young minds are vulnerable to
Pressure to fall in line with any view
Of social ethics which has proved to be
Acceptable to that community.
By such an education people reach
The same philosophies their parents teach.
A generation later they in turn
Will feel obliged to make *their* children learn
The same beliefs, encouraging anew
Unshaken faith that these must all be true.
This is the way religions all contrive
From year to year to keep their faiths alive.

What if we re-evaluate our creeds
To meet our changing and maturing needs?
There'll come a moment when we recognise
We see the world with more perceptive eyes.
Some old conceptions, we must now accept,
Have to be processed through the intellect,
Which, on the evidence of what it finds,
May leave no option but to change our minds.
In this we may appear discourteous
To those who up to now have guided us,
Our parents who well-meaningfully tried
To act as tutor, moralist and guide.
These mentors, whom we trusted in so long,
Could they have actually got it wrong?
See how the pilgrim caravans advance,
Emerging from primeval ignorance!
A billion Christians join the pilgrimage,
A billion Muslims also take the stage,
Their hope is that our species marches on
Towards a better life for everyone,
But still they're parted by the old divides
Which guarantee they keep on taking sides,

Steering two streams of pilgrims hopefully
To separate visions of eternity.
Each one, moreover, splits internally,
Which further dissipates their energy.
They won't acknowledge that their mutual hate
Is now pathetically out of date.
Though all were aiming for a common goal,
Each one believed the future of his soul
Lay in espousing his parental brand,
And changing sides was resolutely banned.
Some cynics say religion seems to be
An outworn bastion of absurdity,
With these two columns in their separate blocks,
Each one convinced that it is orthodox
And that the other faction's destiny
Is to remain a mortal enemy,
Must give more substance to the critics' case
And surely ought to bring us face to face
With the, appalling possibility
That we are marching to catastrophe,
And while our *separate* roads are parallel,
We're making, not for Heaven, but for Hell.

THE POSTVOCALIC 'R'

Poets who still express themselves in rhyme
Are frequently not nearly strict enough.
They just ignore the rule-book all the time,
Hoping to get away with sloppy stuff.
Less choosy poets in the rhyming game,
Taking a simple little word like 'sport',
Rhyme it with words which *nearly* sound the
      same,
Knowing full well they really didn't ort!
We shouldn't rhyme two words if, tiresomely,
Just *one* contains the postvocalic 'R'.
We're victims of the postcode lottery,
Dependent on exactly where we are.
What rhymes in Norwich, York and Golders
      Green
Won't wash in Wigan, Bath or Aberdeen.

RAILWAY GHOSTS

Julia Bradbury's *Railway Walks*

Men like Brunel and Stephenson were seen
As threats to England's green and pleasant land.
The hills and vales where solitude had been
Were ravished by their devastating hand.
Wordsworth and Ruskin bitterly deplored
The desecration of the countryside
When railways threatened what they thought the
    Lord
Had in his wisdom thoughtfully supplied.
But now, when railway lines have had their day,
We have to re-adjust our attitude.
Julia finds a new romantic way
To reach once more that pristine solitude.
Nature and scars of bygone industry
Now blend in new-discover harmony.

THE ROAD AHEAD

See how the leading poets of today
Shake off the chains that held them yesterday,
Tear off the manacles that bound their hands
As they set out to conquer foreign lands.
They clearly choose the challenge to explore
Country where no-one's ever been before.
We harbour no resentment for the youth
Who seek new paths to find poetic truth,
But that's a challenge for a younger mind;
Old men like me prefer to lag behind,
Back on the soil in which our tastes have grown,
Which well-respected poets made their own.
Why should we leave that friendly
    neighbourhood
Just because critics tell us that we should?
The paths that we have followed hitherto
Have led through many places old and new,
Romantic corners, largely unexplored,
In which poetic secrets still are stored.

So, now we've reached the parting of the ways,
Let those who take the highroad earn the praise,
While we enjoy ourselves rooting around
In plots of so-far undiscovered ground,
By which I mean the world of everyday,
Using the tools which they have thrown away.
We'll take the low-road when it is the time;
We'll stride in metre, punctuate in rhyme,
And if you find us sadly out of date,
Stick to the highroad.   It is not too late!

SELF-CONSTRUCTING LANDSCAPES

Watching the sunset and the dying light.
I draw the curtains to shut out the night,
But still I've many windows I can use
To access plenty of rewarding views.
The first of these would be the Internet
Or, failing that, the television set.
Another window, much less obvious,
Frequently proves the most adventurous;
I even use it when I am in bed
Because it's always here within my head.
I start by dredging from my memory
Some well-known place familiar to me,
And then, to get my journey on the go,
I generally choose a route I know.
I start to plan the journey, and the whole
Initially is under my control,
But in a little while I'm satisfied
To hand it over to a nameless guide.
Although I cannot tell you who he is,
I'm confident that guiding hand is his.

I wander through the haunts of yesterday
Until I reach an unfamiliar way,
And with anticipation I explore
Places I never knew about before.
They're peaceful, comfortable, and serene,
Some of the most attractive I have seen.
Old English oakwoods, carpeted with ferns,
Moistened by spray from cool, refreshing burns,
Present an invitation to invade
The tempting pathways through that sylvan
    glade,
And as the path emerges from the wood
A change of scene brings on a change of mood.
Now wider views begin to open out
Over the wilder country round about.
The mossy path gives way to rougher ground
Where massive rock-strewn obstacles abound,
Amorphous blocks of limestone, gleaming white,
Pile on each other with increasing height.
Vertical surfaces with crumbling cracks
Present themselves on isolated stacks,
Only to prove with treacherous deceit
Unstable holds for fingers, hands and feet.

A stomach-churning panic then takes hold.
What if this exploration proves too bold?
What if I am unable to retrace
The steps which brought me to this dreadful
    place?
There, perched above a frightening precipice,
And staring at a bottomless abyss,
I recollect I have an exit plan,
And, waking up, apply it while I can.

SINISTER SENTIMENTS

While *dexter* conjures up efficiency,
For instance in the word 'dexterity',
Sinister takes a very different line,
Meaning suspicious, evil or malign.
Of their initial meanings now bereft
These words no longer stand for right and left.
Sinister hints at the perfidious,
The false, the crafty and the treacherous.
Like others I've interpreted the word
As meaning what those adjectives inferred.
Sadly my Latin withered long ago,
But still I should have had the sense to know
That, though the public failed to see the light,
It just means 'left', the opposite of 'right',
And though I clearly knew that I was wrong,
I quite uncritically went along
With those who quite erroneously had
Interpreted the word as meaning 'bad'.
Early one August morning I awoke
To find I'd been afflicted by a stroke.

At first I didn't really understand
Just why I couldn't move my foot or hand,
Or why those healthy muscles on the right
Were unaffected by this neural blight.
It wasn't long before it dawned on me;
Dexter rewarded my consistency
In always using it with deference
As a distinctive mark of excellence,
While *Sinister* in animosity
Was now in anger getting back at me!

STAGECRAFT

As each emerges from that waiting-room,
The sheltered refuge of our mother's womb,
We find a play in progress on the stage
Which tells the story of our heritage.
The *dramatis personae* of the play
Have told the story up to yesterday,
And we, to understand the present act,
Have got to recognise this simple fact:
The characters that they appear to be
Are products of a previous history,
And through the earlier chapters of the play
They have emerged as who they are today.
We cannot change, however hard we try,
The things that happened in the days gone by,
But knowing them will help us understand
How to progress the business now in hand.
Into this picture-frame we try to fit
Innumerable pieces bit by bit,
And, sure enough, we shortly start to find
That, when adjacent pieces are combined,

Parts of the jigsaw now appear to be
Emerging fragments of reality.
The time will come with our advancing age
To make our final exit from the stage
And leave it for the actors of the day
To make new contributions to the play.

STOKE POGES CHURCHYARD

The curfew tolls the knell of parting day;
The lowing herd winds slowly o'er the lea.
The ploughman wants a word with Mr Gray
About the present actuality.

Although the churchyard hasn't altered much,
At least not since the eighteenth century,
I guess he'd now be talking Double Dutch
About its overbuilt periphery.

With rows of little houses everywhere
And roars of traffic on the motorway,
Frustrated drivers tearing out their hair
And Heathrow less than seven miles away,

If Thomas Gray could come and see it now,
Surrounded by suburban buildings and,
Knowing what Betjeman had said of Slough,
The self-promoted pride of Metroland,

He would be horrified at what we've done
With England's most iconic rural scene,
And have a barrelful of harmless fun
Contrasting it with what it might have been.

Happily remnants of rusticity
In England still contrive to find a place,
Fragments of pastoral antiquity
Which brash modernity cannot efface.

As for the Elegy, he wrote it when
Those acres still were underneath the plough.
If he could call it 'elegiac ' then,
What would he think of to describe it now?

THE SYCAMORE TREES

We've strolled through the country, Amanda
    and I,
And the morning is bright, not a cloud in the
    sky.
We have just had a break and are taking our
    ease
Enjoying the shade of some sycamore trees.
This commonplace tree's not as widely admired
As those beautiful trees which have always
    inspired
Our poets and painters and sensitive folk,
Like the holly, the willow, the elm and the oak.
But now it's this *acer* which comes to our aid
And casts a penumbra of welcoming shade.
We shun the temptation of settling down
For it's time to press on to the fringe of the
    town.
We turn for a moment and gratefully seize
A quick backward glance at the sycamore trees.
The traffic gets noisy; it's crowding the street,
The sidewalk is pounded by scurrying feet.

The buildings get closer and dauntingly high;
They threaten to strangle the view of the sky.
But through a small gap there is just room to
    squeeze
A faraway glimpse of those sycamore trees.
The farther we travel the more do we find
How tiny they've grown as we leave them
    behind.
Municipal buildings are all very well
And, yes, for a time we fall under their spell,
But sooner or later we're feeling unease;
We are fast losing touch with the sycamore trees.
Amanda's not worried; she thinks it's OK;
Our bonding with nature has now had its day.
The lights of the city are stronger by far
Than even the brightest celestial star.
I'm fond of Amanda.   I like her a lot,
But now she's in danger of losing the plot.
If trees are restricting the growth of the town
Her remedy's simple; you just chop 'em down!
Amanda is one of those people who think
The town and the country should sever the link.

She couldn't be bothered to put up a fight
In defence of a cause she must know to be right.
She'll throw in the towel if 'Progress' decrees
And meekly abandon the sycamore trees.
But *me*, I shall side with the advocates who
Are equally pledged to the opposite view.
The friends of Amanda are winning the day.
All over the world they are chipping away
At whatever is left of the countryside now
In the acres which used to be under the plough.
The impotent public capitulates and
With minimum protest surrenders the land.
While 'Natural England' is doing its best
To soften the blow by protecting the rest,
Rapacious developers proudly proclaim
That total replacement's the name of the game.
When sound conservation is brought to its knees
It's jolly bad luck for the sycamore trees.
They're not very posh and they're not very rare
So they're not very special; it's just that they're
    there!
It isn't the function of leaves in the trees
To summon the pollen-distributing bees,

But verdant florescence would never be seen
If set in a matrix of monochrome green;
So flowers make use of more brilliant hues,
Like reds, pinks and purples and yellows and
    blues.
This prompts us to ask of those sycamores,
    'Why
Should they now be successful in catching the
    eye?'
They're one of the commonest trees in the wood
And no-one could claim they're outstandingly
    good,
But when everything else is of concrete or brick
A sharp colour contrast may still do the trick.
With building materials running the game
The balance of colour will not be the same,
So the merest suggestion of chlorophyll green
May well catch the eye in this urbanised scene.
The horses have bolted!   Perhaps it's too late
For the simple precaution of barring the gate.
But one thing's for certain, and this is a fact,
It's time we believers got in on the act.

Amanda and I have decided to part;
I don't think she really had nature at heart.
So farewell, Amanda. It's easy to see
On this delicate subject we'd never agree.
But every so often remember me, please,
When you sit in the shadow of sycamore trees.

SYNAESTHESIA

The several senses that we can employ
To bring us an experience of joy
We obstinately try to keep apart
Within their own exclusive kinds of art.
The things that we encounter through our eyes
We look for in our picture galleries.
We'd not expect to find the sounds we hear
Artistically represented there.
Images which are purely visual
We wouldn't look for in the concert hall,
But if it is the auditory sense
Initiating the experience,
It's there that we would find its artistry
Rather than in the picture gallery.
We cannot see what Mozart has to do
With Rembrandt, Cuyp or Caravaggio,
Nor shall we ever have the chance to see
Unless we look at it more carefully.

Enquiring pioneers like Jane Mackay [2]
Have taken it upon themselves to try,
Through diligent experiments, to find
How they are functionally intertwined.
Within our brains some neural gossamer
Must somehow link the things we see and hear,
And those who have the courage to explore
In art and music what they're looking for
Begin to throw an unexpected light
On how two different artforms may unite
And thus attain a synaesthetic goal,
Blending them in one integrated whole.

---

[2] A South London doctor who gave up her practice to found *Sounding Art.*

TO VOTE OR NOT TO VOTE

The public has one fatal flaw, and this
Is its unreasonable prejudice.
One of the things which really gets its goat
Is giving prisoners the right to vote.
If they are pressed to give a reason why,
'They've forfeited their right!' is their reply.
'They should have thought about the
    consequence
'Before they went committing an offence!'
It's understandable to think that they
Might well react in this simplistic way,
But those who take the time to think it through
May reach a more enlightened point of view.
Those we commit to prison are inclined
To get in a rebellious frame of mind.
They see themselves as a minority
Excluded from polite society,
And, faced by critical opinion,
They look for pegs to hang their anger on.

They search for some illogicality
In the contempt of the majority.
For them the well-behaved community
Is bound to represent the enemy
And any gesture of exclusion thus
Contributes to the sense of 'them and us'.
It follows that we shouldn't be surprised
If they perceive themselves as ostracised.
Small wonder, therefore, if it comes to pass
That we create 'a feral underclass'!
These are the criminals who trash the town,
The arsonists who burn the buildings down.
In our society we judge success
By the material assets we possess,
For some to profit, others have to fail,
And these are always bringing up the tail.
They're angry that they've never had a say
In framing laws which had them put away,
And, conscious that the system is unfair,
They find this final insult hard to bear.
I have to say the chances are remote
That, if they exercise the right to vote,

They'll be a threat to the stability
Of parliamentary democracy.
To say it's something they're not fit to do
Is fuelling hostility anew.
It must be in our interest to see
They're reinstated in society.
Voting's a privilege undoubtedly,
But also a responsibility,
A civic duty, which, to our dismay,
Has ceased to motivate the youth today.
There surely is some inconsistency
If we deny to this minority
The rights and privileges to enjoy
Which we encourage others to employ.
We mustn't be irresolute in this,
But fight against the public prejudice
And give repentant sinners cause to see
They're not excluded from the family.

TRAGIC HEROINES

A gritstone moorland, lonely, bleak and bare,
Stretches between the Calder and the Aire.
Above the valley of the River Worth,
Before it joins with Airedale in the north,
Two gaunt reminders of a bygone age,
The parish church and Haworth Parsonage,
On the high ground above the valley stand,
Surveying what we know as 'Brontëland'.
Such was the sisters' literary fame,
They gave the landscape their illustrious name.
These famous daughters of the Parsonage
All perished at a very early age.
Emily, in creating Catherine,
Gave us another tragic heroine,
Who also, in the novel, sadly died,
Her injudicious love unsatisfied.
Turn the clock forward to the present day.
Turn your feet south along the Pennine Way,
Take in the moorland landscape as you go
Until you see the Calder down below.

Another churchyard now comes into sight
On yet another dominating height,
And we discover, as we wander in,
The tombstone of another heroine.
Like Cathy Earnshaw and like Emily,
She too had met with early tragedy.
Herself a poet and a poet's wife,
Confused and in despair, she took her life.
Her loyal followers were quick to name
Her poet husband as the one to blame.
When first I heard the story I inclined
To harbour only anger in my mind.
How could she leave that pair of infant mites,
Depriving them of their dependant rights
To love, protection and parental care
To get her own back for a love affair?
For what she did I'm no apologist,
But she deserves a neutral annalist.
When we discover more about the facts
They throw more light on how a person acts.
And, on reflection, it was clear her pain
Imposed a quite intolerable strain.

Only read *Daddy* and you'll get a clue
To what poor Sylvia had been going through.
Mentally sick, and too confused to think,
Hughes's desertion pushed her past the brink,
And, like some creature she could not control,
Blind desperation duly took its toll.
It now seems pretty evident to me
He'd treated Sylvia pretty shamefully.
Whatever protestations he had made,
Sylvia must have felt herself betrayed.
Yet it's apparent from the aftermath
Hughes never freed himself from Sylvia Plath.
The poems and the letters which they wrote
Strike an ambiguous, confusing note,
Which in a curious way reminded me
Of that strange man dreamt up by Emily.
Banishing reason from his fevered mind,
And leaving all reality behind,
Heathcliff, obsessed with Cathy to the end,
Nursed a fierce passion for his childhood friend.
Unable to escape his lovelorn past,
He kept alive that passion to the last.

I know no reason to explain at all
Why Plath's remains should rest at Heptonstall,
Yet, in the public eye, that came to be
The stark reminder of her tragedy.
As pointed out by her biographers,
It was *his* patch but never really *hers.*
Her poems make it very clear that she
Found little comfort in that scenery.
A resting-place more likely to inspire
Was Tawton, which she loved, in Devonshire.
Ted's first two loves horrifically died
In cold, premeditated suicide.
One daughter, on the threshold of her life,
Had perished, murdered by his would-be wife.
Ted's enemies, to their eternal shame,
Went on to desecrate the poet's name.
With chisels they removed it from her stone,
Leaving the name of Sylvia alone.
Like Heathcliff, Hughes could never leave
    behind
Sylvia's image in his troubled mind.
Mixed sentiments of anger, love and hate
Conspired to haunt the Poet Laureate.

Even the healing power of poetry
Could not release him from his agony.
Poets can't be expected to avoid
Such pain as plagued the lad from
    Mytholmroyd.
Now every time it figures in the news
It seems to us the hapless House of Hughes
Has more than had its melancholy share
Of pitiable tragedies to bear,
As if ordained to be calamitous,
A sort of modern House of Atreus,
Whence came the names in those now-famous
    lists,
Coined by Victorian psychologists,
Of neurasthenic abnormalities:
Electra, Oedipus and such as these.
Though it was something Ted was not to see,
After another half a century,
Tragedy was repeated, and we find
That little boy Sylvia left behind
In the next generation carried on
The saga that his mother had begun.

Though taking him to scientific fame,
His tragic story ended just the same.
Accepting his incompetence to cope,
He closed his struggle with a length of rope.
Sylvia and Ted were surely equally
The victims of this lovers' tragedy.
Now that they're dead isn't it time to find
A way to leave the bickering behind?
Give them at last their ultimate release
And leave their memories to rest in peace.
No more recriminations, taking sides
On who must answer for those suicides!
For me the moorland's vast, expansive views
Encapsulate the lives of Plath and Hughes.
The painful, smouldering embers that remain
Of a communion of love and pain
Are mirrored in that moor of Millstone Grit
And those sad graves at either end of it.

VERSIFICATION

'Poetry' is a controversial name.
Poets and versifiers aren't the same.
It's never been my ultimate desire
To reach those heights to which the first aspire.
I just present the things of everyday
In a more systematic, rhythmic way,
Accessible to simple folk like me,
Far from the cutting edge of poetry!
We're not in competition for the fame
Which honours the distinguished poet's name,
But, well contented in obscurity,
We cling to well-tried rules of prosody.
We know that's certain to infuriate
Critics who think of us as out-of-date.
They say to call us 'poets' is absurd;
That 'versifiers' is the proper word,
And, contrary to what you might expect,
I will concede they're possibly correct.
Such critics think the rules of prosody
Are a sure sign of mediocrity

And poets who engage with them are prone
To finish in the relegation zone.
To plumb the secrets of philosophy
Requires the skills of proper poetry,
While self-assessment in psychology
Is far beyond the reach of folk like me.
We versifiers are supposed to stick
To simple formats, like the limerick.
Given the chance, though, we will never fail
To aim a little higher up the scale,
And if we cannot judge how far to go
That's when the tensions may begin to show.
If versifiers can't keep in their place
They'll soon discover what they have to face.
Their foes are sure to make a song and dance
To punish their confounded arrogance.
The critics' columns in the serious press
Will teach ambitious wordsmiths not to mess!
Remember, if your poem reads like prose
It's probable you've joined the ranks of those
Who have discovered how to play the game
That took them to the pinnacle of fame.

Too much self-confidence will never do;
Too little, and they'll never notice you.
There is no obvious criterion
That tells you how to know which side you're
    on,
But better that you know the difference
Than run the risk of giving them offence.
Whether you make the poet's grade or not,
You should make sure you're in your proper
    slot.
There is a very easy way to see
If what you write is proper poetry.
Should the distinction still remain in doubt,
Just read these lines and you will soon find out!

VILLANELLE

To Brian Newbould, who, in a clever villanelle,
challenged me to reply in like mode.

I can't imagine why the hell
My fellow bard is moved to say
I ought to write a villanelle.

His challenge doesn't ring a bell,
So why, I ask, should I obey?
I can't imagine why the hell!

I am a novice, truth to tell,
So why should he expect me, pray,
To write a flipping villanelle?

I have, alas, no magic spell,
No elegiac ace to play.
I can't imagine why the hell!

To think that I could do it well
Is quite a compliment to pay,
So should I write a villanelle?

What are these urges which impel
My learned friend to think this way?
This poem should suffice to tell
I *cannot* write a villanelle!

VOWEL-CREEP

Time was when we pronounced the letter 'u'
Like its close relative, the double 'o',
Shaping the lips as if to whistle through.
Only the Welsh denied that this was so.

The younger generation came along
And, brandishing their own authority,
Insisted that we all had got it wrong,
And moved the sound towards a double 'e'.

The Evening News became 'The Evening Knees'.
The harvest moon became 'the harvest meen'.
The verb 'to choose' became the verb 'to cheese'.
The afternoon is now 'the afterneen'.

Why can't we leave our vowels as they were?
I hate to see my native tongue 'abeesed',
But still I wouldn't want to cause a stir.
I just give up.   I'm totally 'confeesed.

It's no damned 'yeese' denying it is so.

'U' has become a victim of 'abeese'

And we supporters of the *status quo*

Have to admit we've met our 'Waterlees'!

WARS OF THE ROSES

Not long ago the Labour Party chose
An icon for its 'New' identity.
A picture of a perfect English rose
Now symbolises party unity.
They never told the public who it was
Who chose that controversial colour, red.
We think he came from Manchester, because,
If not he must be potty in the head!
To those of us who live beyond the Trent
The Field of Bosworth was but yesterday.
East of the Pennines people still resent
The Tudor Rose.   It's *white* that's still O.K.
Didn't they know they would infuriate
The Yorkshire half of the electorate?

WELCOME DECEPTION

To David Cook, artist.

Can long-lost places come to life again?
Thanks to a painter's skilful artistry
The two dimensions of a picture-plane
Are magically now restored to three.
I seem to see the tree-girt church at Cley.
I know, of course, it isn't there at all.
A film of tinctured oil, smoothed out to dry,
Is what now decorates my parlour wall.
Come, kind deception.   Whisk me far away
Back to my childhood's land of lost content.
Turn back the clock to scenes of yesterday
And hours presumed irrevocably spent.
How gladly is the fallacy believed!
How willingly the grateful eye deceived!

THE WIDOWER

His privilege had been to find a wife
Who shared his passion for the outdoor life.
It was their joy, over the hills and vales,
To walk through Scotland, Cumbria and Wales.
The road which led through more than
    threescore years
Eventually reached a Vale of Tears,
But, breaking through a barrier of pain,
Led to a way to find those years again.
All sorts of places he had come to know
And fall in love with all those years ago
Now decorate his humble cottage walls
With far horizons, hills and waterfalls.
Although his partner is no longer here
She regularly seems to come and share
Images of that mountain scenery
Which lie recorded in his memory.
No longer can he walk the hills, and yet
The television and the Internet
Recall from the recesses of his mind
Pictures that Father Time has left behind.

Enlisting virtual reality,

He challenges his incapacity.

The close confinement of his little room,

Far from encouraging a sense of gloom,

Affords a novel opportunity

For exploration and discovery

With unexpected chances to attain

Places he thought he'd never see again.

Far from lamenting an unhappy lot,

He counts the blessings he's already got,

And for his old but still enquiring eyes

This is the place in which his future lies.

WIGAN PIER

Cruising along this tranquil waterway,
One sees a landscape of gentility;
Opulent residences there today
Look out on an idyllic scenery.
Wetlands and lakes among sporadic trees
Invite the duck, the goose, the graceful swan,
And make a pretty picture out of these
For eager visitors to gaze upon.
The 'Wigan Flashes' border the canal,
Scotsman's and Turner's, Pearson's, Horrocks',
   Bryn,
Westwood and Ochre are their names, and all
Enhance the landscape they're located in.
Reedbed and mossland, willow-carr and peat
Create varieties of habitat
Where fen- and water-loving birds can meet
And twitchers watch to see what they are at.
Here is a haven of rusticity,
Yet Orwell found, less than a mile from here,
In dereliction and obscurity,
That legendary icon, Wigan Pier.

His grim portrayal of that cheerless scene
Back in the 'Thirties, when he wrote his book,
Seems to be what he thought it *should* have
    been,
How, I suspect, he *wanted* it to look.
Surely he must have laid it on too thick
When he described its grinding poverty,
Lambasting with his left-wing rhetoric
His picture of a sick society!
His Leeds and Liverpool Canal was black
With coal-dust and industrial debris.
For him the slums of Poolstock turned their
    back
On nature as it really ought to be.
Women conversing in the treeless street
Seemed to be part and parcel of the place.
Shawls wrapped their heads and clogs confined
    their feet;
Premature aging showed in every face.
This was the Lancashire of yesterday
With Kirkless Ironworks half way up the hill,
Watching a dirty Douglas sneak its way
Past gasworks, colliery and cotton mill.

This was the Empire overlorded by
The Wigan Coal and Iron Company,
Which was in Orwell's unforgiving eye
The author of its inhumanity.
How can we reconcile these images,
The one a charming, quite enchanting sight,
The other, urban slums and ugliness?
Are they both wrong, or could they both be
    right?
Within those limpid lakes the evidence
To solve this puzzling riddle may be found;
They're *both* the products of that subsidence
That dominated everything around.
Beauty allegedly is just skin-deep;
Remedy was at hand, but had to wait.
Not till the mining had been put to sleep
Could landscape surgeons start to operate.
Suspend your sceptic's disbelief, because
Orwell's descriptive words were all too fair.
That's how the south of Wigan really was.
How do I know?   I saw it.   I was there!

OTHER POEMS BY JAY APPLETON.

The following collections are in print (2011) and may be obtained from the publishers, Wildhern Press, Unit 22, Horcott Industrial Estate, Horcott Road, Fairford, Glos, GL7 4BX, or from booksellers.

Grains Among the Chaff (2000/8),
ISBN 978-1-84830-074-3 *
The Cottingham Collection (2001/8),
ISBN 978-1-84830-075-0
A Love Affair with Landscape (2009),
ISBN 978-1-84830-098-9
Shadows of the Evening (2009),
ISBN 978-1-84830-206-8
Enter the Fat Lady (2009),
ISBN 978-1- 84830-207-5 *
The Good, the Bad and the Ugly: a Meta-Aesthetic
    Extravaganza (2010),
ISBN 978-1-84830-263-1

*   With illustrations by Geoffrey Shovelton

NORFOLK DIALECT STORIES ON DVD

Stories from East Anglia, originally written and read in dialect by Jay Appleton to mark the opening of the BBC Norwich Studios in 1958, now read (2009) by David Woodward.   Two-set DVD for 'Friends of Norfolk Dialect' from Stewart Orr Sound Services, Prior's Croft Barn, Mendham, Harleston, Norfolk, IP20 0JG.

Lightning Source UK Ltd.
Milton Keynes UK
UKOW050115131211

183655UK00001B/2/P